9/20

MINDFUL MENTALITY

RESPECT

BY AMBER BULLIS, MLIS

BLUE OWL
BOOKS

TIPS FOR CAREGIVERS

Social and emotional learning (SEL) helps children connect with their emotions and gain a better understanding of themselves. Mindfulness can support this learning and help them develop a kind and inclusive mentality. By incorporating mindfulness and SEL into early learning, students can establish this mentality early and be better equipped to build strong connections and communities.

BEFORE READING

Talk to the reader about respect.

Discuss: What does respect mean to you? How do you show it? How do people respect you?

AFTER READING

Talk to the reader about what he or she learned about respect from this book.

Discuss: What are some other ways you can show respect? Have you ever felt disrespected? How did it make you feel?

SEL GOAL

Increasing self-awareness can increase self-respect. Have students think about a person they respect. Have them write a list of traits that person has that they respect. Then have them write a list of their own traits. Ask students to compare the two lists. Which traits are similar? Which traits are different? How can they work to show the traits they respect?

TABLE OF CONTENTS

CHAPTER 1

WHAT IS RESPECT?

Min is Kelsey and Kayla's new neighbor. She is from a different country and speaks another language. She is different from Kelsey and Kayla, but they all belong in their **community**.

Kelsey and Kayla learn to say "hello" in Min's language. They practice saying it. They learn about Min's **culture**, too. This is one way to show respect!

Being respectful shows others that they matter. It is important to respect others, no matter how similar or different they are from you. Why? This creates happier and stronger communities! Everyone deserves to feel safe and like they belong.

GOLDEN RULE

Have you ever heard of the Golden Rule? It means to treat others how you would like to be treated. Showing respect follows the Golden Rule. How do you follow this rule?

Showing respect can sometimes be hard. You might feel **disrespected**. Your feelings are hurt. What can you do if you feel disrespected? First, take some deep breaths. This can help you calm down. Then be **mindful**. How? Ask yourself how you are feeling and why.

Maybe it is hard to show respect when you don't understand the other person. Ask that person questions. Get to know him or her.

CHAPTER 2

RESPECTING OTHERS

Lin wants to watch a scary movie. Sal doesn't like scary movies. They have different interests. That is OK. Instead of arguing, they **compromise**. They respect each other's interests and watch a movie they both like!

Gia is upset and crying. Britt wants to give her a hug, but she asks first. Britt respects Gia's **personal space**.

Jack respects his classmates. How? He raises his hand. He waits for his teacher to call on him before he speaks. He listens to his classmates' ideas. He does not talk while they are talking.

Jack respects his teacher, too. Why? She is in charge while he is at school. He listens to her directions. He is kind and polite to her.

RESPECTING ELDERS

You might hear someone ask you to respect your elders. This means to show respect to people who are older than you. Why? Older people have more experience. Ask adults you trust for **advice**. They have your best interests at heart!

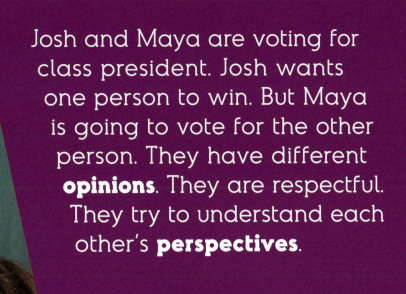

Josh and Maya are voting for class president. Josh wants one person to win. But Maya is going to vote for the other person. They have different **opinions**. They are respectful. They try to understand each other's **perspectives**.

You can respect more than just people. Jo respects places and things. She loves the library in her school. She is careful with her books. She returns them on time.

RESPECT EARTH

You can also treat Earth with respect. How? Use less water. Turn lights off when you leave a room. Bring your own bags to the grocery store. Can you think of other ways to respect Earth?

CHAPTER 3

SELF-RESPECT

You can respect yourself, too! **Self-respect** builds **confidence**. Jana tried hard. But she made a mistake. She is **patient** with herself. She knows she needs time to learn!

Self-respect includes **accepting** yourself. No one is perfect. Everyone has strengths and weaknesses. This is OK! Part of self-respect is knowing what you are good at and what you might need help with.

Respect your body. Treat it with **compassion**. How can you do this? Be mindful and check in with yourself often. See how your body is feeling. Are you hungry? Find a healthy snack. Do you feel tired? Get extra sleep. Self-respect is giving your body what it needs.

Everyone deserves to be respected! How can you show respect today?

GOALS AND TOOLS

GROW WITH GOALS

There are many ways to show respect. Try these goals!

Goal: Think of people you respect. Why do you respect them? Write down ways that they show respect to others.

Goal: Using manners is one way to show respect. Choose a day to focus on saying please, thank you, and you're welcome.

Goal: Be a role model. Others will learn how to be respectful when they see you treating people with respect.

MINDFULNESS EXERCISE

Feeling down about yourself? Mindfulness can help you build self-respect!

1. Think about yourself. What do you like about yourself? Think positively!

2. Reflect on your positive traits. Write them down as a list.

3. Put that list in a place where you will see it each day.

4. When you see the list, stop and read it slowly. Think about each trait. Reflect on what you like about yourself and why.

GLOSSARY

accepting
Agreeing that something is correct, satisfactory, or enough.

advice
A suggestion about what someone should do.

community
A group of people who all have something in common.

compassion
A feeling of sympathy for and a desire to help someone who is suffering.

compromise
To agree to accept something that is not entirely what you wanted in order to satisfy some of the requests of other people.

confidence
A feeling of self-assuredness and a strong belief in your own abilities.

culture
The ideas, customs, traditions, and way of life of a group of people.

disrespected
Showed a lack of respect.

mindful
A mentality achieved by focusing on the present moment and calmly recognizing and accepting your feelings, thoughts, and sensations.

opinions
People's personal feelings about people and things.

patient
Able to put up with problems or delays without getting angry or upset.

personal space
The space immediately surrounding someone.

perspectives
Particular attitudes toward or ways of looking at things.

self-respect
Respect for oneself.

TO LEARN MORE

Finding more information is as easy as 1, 2, 3.

1. Go to www.factsurfer.com

2. Enter "**respect**" into the search box.

3. Choose your cover to see a list of websites.

INDEX

Blue Owl Books are published by Jump!, 5357 Penn Avenue South, Minneapolis, MN 55419, www.jumplibrary.com

Copyright © 2021 Jump! International copyright reserved in all countries. No part of this book may be reproduced in any form without written permission from the publisher.

Library of Congress Cataloging-in-Publication Data

Names: Bullis, Amber, author.
Title: Respect / by Amber Bullis.
Description: Minneapolis: Jump!, Inc., [2021] | Series: Mindful mentality
Includes index. | Audience: Ages 7–10 | Audience: Grades 2–3
Identifiers: LCCN 2019055002 (print)
LCCN 2019055003 (ebook)
ISBN 9781645273899 (library binding)
ISBN 9781645273905 (paperback)
ISBN 9781645273912 (ebook)
Subjects: LCSH: Respect–Juvenile literature. | Values–Juvenile literature.
Classification: LCC BJ1533.R4 B85 2021 (print)
LCC BJ1533.R4 (ebook) | DDC 179/.9–dc23
LC record available at https://lccn.loc.gov/2019055002
LC ebook record available at https://lccn.loc.gov/2019055003

Editor: Jenna Gleisner
Designer: Molly Ballanger

Photo Credits: Majorosl66/Dreamstime, cover; Kemter/iStock, 1; Zinkevych/iStock, 3; gpointstudio/iStock, 4, 5 (foreground); Mark Baldwin/Shutterstock, 5 (background); kali9/iStock, 6–7; fstop123/iStock, 8–9; Syda Productions/Shutterstock, 10; Myrleen Pearson/Alamy, 11; Monkey Business Images/Shutterstock, 12–13, 20–21; TongRo Images/Alamy, 14–15; Kenishirotie/iStock, 16–17; vgajic/iStock, 18; OJO Images/iStock, 19.

Printed in the United States of America at Corporate Graphics in North Mankato, Minnesota.